# AIRLINE

# BOEIN

**Acknowledgements**  I would like to thank friends Ralf Braun and Iain Logan for their assistance. All photographs taken by the author are on Kodachrome 64 film.

First published in the UK in 1995 by
Airlife Publishing Ltd

**British Library Cataloguing in Publication Data**
A catalogue record for this book is available from the British Library

ISBN 1 85310 536 8

Typeset by Litho Link Ltd, Welshpool, Powys, Wales
Printed in Hong Kong

# Airlife Publishing Ltd

101 Longden Road, Shrewsbury SY3 9EB

# Introduction

For the past few decades the Boeing Airplane Company has, without doubt, been the most successful manufacturer of commercial aircraft, particularly since the introduction of the jet era. The Boeing 707 can be claimed to be the aircraft which changes transatlantic travel whilst the 727 became the world's best-selling airliner. That record has since been lost but, to another Boeing product, the 737, which at the time of writing has amassed an amazing 3,053 orders, 2,650 of which have been delivered. The success of the 747 Jumbo is legendary, but two other Boeing products, the 757 and 767 are also selling extremely well.

On 14 July 1978 Boeing announced that it was to proceed with the manufacture of the twin-engined 767 model following an order from United Airlines for thirty aircraft. Developed simultaneously with the 757, the 767 was aimed primarily at transcontinental and intercontinental routes. In appearance the 767 is similar to the Airbus A-300, powered by two wing mounted turbofan engines, and the customer has a choice of General Electric, Pratt & Whitney or Rolls-Royce engines. The wide body fuselage has twin-aisles with seven abreast seating in a 2x3x2 configuration, though this is often increased to 2x4x2 in charter configuration. The 767 is assembled in a new building adjoining the 747 assembly hangar at Boeing's Everett plant, which shares the runway with Paine Field/Snohomish County airport. The basic model is designated the 767-200, and the prototype was rolled out on 4 August 1981 with the first flight on 26 September, five months ahead of the 757 which is produced at Renton.

By this time United had increased its order to thirty-nine aircraft, with options for a further thirty, whilst other major US carriers Delta and American and TWA had ordered substantial numbers and the Boeing salesmen were rubbing their hands in anticipation. By the end of 1981 Boeing had received 173 orders for the 767, with options on a further 138. These included orders from across the border in Canada from Air Canada and Pacific Western, while All Nippon became the first Asian customer. Britannia Airways became the first European and also the first charter airline to select the type, followed quickly by Norway's Braathens. Inroads were made to South America when Colombia's Avianca joined those on the order book. Alarm bells rang briefly in June 1982 when United cancelled and deferred orders for twenty of those aircraft on order due to the effects of recession in the US airline industry. Two months later, on 19 August, United took delivery of the first production aircraft which was soon pressed into service on the Chicago–Denver route, replacing fuel-thirsty DC-10s.

On 6 March 1984 the next variant, the 767-200ER, flew for the first time. This aircraft features a higher gross weight and increased fuel capacity due to wing centre-section tanks, permitting a significant increase in range to over 4,000nm (6,000km). First recipient of this variant was Ethiopian Airlines, the first 767 order from the African continent. The availability of the -200ER encouraged a number of airlines, including American and United to transfer some of their orders to the newer variant. In 1986 the 767-200ER set two new world records. The first being a new world distance record of 6,854nm set during the delivery of a Kuwait Airways aircraft from Seattle direct to the capital of the small Arab country. This was followed five months later when a Lan-Chile aircraft made the first scheduled commercial crossing of the Atlantic by a twin-jet aircraft, completing the flight from Rio de Janeiro to Madrid in ten hours and twelve minutes.

In 1983 Boeing announced that a stretched variant known as the series -300 was to be produced, two fuselage plugs increasing the length by 6.43m (21ft 1in), increasing capacity by thirty-seven in maximum configuration. The first of this variant was delivered to Japan Airlines in September 1985, with competitor All Nippon taking delivery nearly two years later. The series -300ER extended range variant first flew on 19 December 1986, with American Airlines the first customer where the type was put to use on the increasing number of transatlantic routes. American Airlines is currently the largest 767 operator with a total of sixty-seven aircraft in use with a further four on order. Fellow US airlines Delta and United were quick to follow suit in introducing the -300ER to their fleets.

The 767 family of aircraft, particularly the -300 variants, is proving increasingly popular with European charter airlines due to its exceptional range and high density seating. There is however quite a disparity in seating capacity amongst European charter airlines. Whereas airlines such as Condor, LTU and Spanair seat less than the often quoted capacity of 290, UK operators Airtours and Leisure International cram in an amazing 326 and 327 passengers respectively. On the series -200 aircraft 200 passengers is the maximum capacity in mixed configuration, while 290 can be seated on single-class charter flights.

One of the attractions of the 767 is its ETOPS (Extended Twin Operations) capability which makes it an ideal choice for those who operate the aircraft across the Atlantic. Such is the reliability of modern airliners and engines that the 767 has been instrumental in changing the rules applicable to twin-engined aircraft operating long-haul flights over water – ETOPS. Previously these twin-engined aircraft had to fly circuitous routes that would keep them within one hour's flight of an airport in case of the loss of an engine, a rule that does not apply to three and four-engined aircraft. However the reliability of aircraft like the Boeing 757, 767 and Airbus A-310 convinced the authorities that this should be extended to two hours. This approval was originally restricted to 767s powered by Pratt & Whitney JT9D-7R4 engines, however this approval was soon extended to General Electric CF6-80A and Rolls-Royce RB211-535E engines. There are now a number of airframe/engine combinations and operators approved for ETOPS, many of which are now cleared for flight three hours from land.

In 1995 the latest 767 variant will take to the air, this being the -300ER freighter for United Parcel Service who have ordered an initial batch of thirty, with options for a further thirty.

Boeing recently announced that production of the -200 variant has ceased, but there is no doubt that the popular -300 will remain in production for a number of years yet and, at the time of writing, over 500 767s have been delivered to over seventy airlines world-wide.

The following either operate or have the Boeing 767 on order. Those in brackets no longer operate it, or indeed no longer exist. (Aer Lingus), (Aero Maritime), Aeroflot, Aeromexico, (Aero-Peru), Air Algerie, (Air Aruba), Air Caledonie International, Air Canada, Air China, Air Europe Italy, Air France, (Air Holland), Air Mauritius, Air New Zealand, Air Pacific, Air Seychelles, (Air Tanzania), Air Zimbabwe, Airtours International, All Nippon Airways, American Airlines, American Trans Air, Ansett Australia Airlines, Asiana, (Australia Asia), Avianca, Balkan Bulgarian Airlines, (Braathens), Britannia Airways, British Airways, (C.A.A.C.), Canadian Airlines International, (China Airlines), China Southern Airlines, Condor, Continental Airlines, Delta Airlines, Egyptair, El Al, Ethiopian Airlines, EVA Air, Gulf Air, Japan Airlines, Japan

Transocean Air, Japanese Air Self-Defence Force, Kazakhstan Airlines, K.L.M., Kuwait Airways, LAN-Chile, Lauda Air Spa, Leisure International Airways, L.A.M., L.O.T., (L.T.U.), L.T.U. Sud, Malev, Martinair, Olympic Airways, (Pacific Western), (Piedmont), Polynesian Airlines, (Pluna), Qantas, (Qatari Airlines), (Region Air), Royal Brunei Airlines, S.A.S. Shanghai Airlines, Sobelair, South African Airlines, (Southwest Airlines, Japan), Spanair, T.A.C.A. T.A.E.S.A., Transaero, TransBrasil, T.W.A., United Airlines, United Parcel Service, USAir, Varig, Vietnam Airlines, World Air Network.

## SPECIFICATIONS

|  | –200 | –200ER |
|---|---|---|
| First flight date: | 26 September 1981 | 6 March 1984 |
| Max. accommodation: | 290 | 290 |
| Wing span: | 47.57m (156ft 1in) | 47.57m (156ft 1in) |
| Length: | 48.51m (159ft 2in) | 48.51m (159ft 2in) |
| Height: | 15.85m (52ft) | 15.85m (52ft) |
| Max. t/o weight: | 142,881kg (315,000lb) | 175,540kg (387,000lb) |
| Range with max. pax: | 7,135km (3,850nm) | 12,611km (7,836nm) |
| Max. cruising speed: | Mach 0.80 | Mach 0.80 |

|  | -300 | -300ER |
|---|---|---|
| First flight date: | 30 January 1986 | 19 December 1986 |
| Max. accommodation: | 327 | 327 |
| Wing span: | 47.57m (156ft 1in) | 47.57m (156ft 1in) |
| Length: | 54.94m (180ft 3in) | 54.94m (180ft 3in) |
| Height: | 15.85m (52ft) | 15.85 (52ft) |
| Max. t/o weight: | 175,540kg (387,000lb) | 184,640kg (407,000lb) |
| Range with max. pax: | 7,895km (4,260nm) | 11,230km (6,060nm) |
| Max. cruising speed: | Mach 0.80 | Mach 0.80 |

## AER LINGUS (EI/EIN)

The Irish national carrier is a long-established operator of Boeing products, and is one of the few airlines which can boast it has operated every variant of the 737. Long-haul routes have been operated by ageing 747s, though these are currently being replaced by Airbus A-330s, whilst Saab SF340s and Fokker 50s are used on domestic and some UK regional services. Early in 1991 Aer Lingus took delivery of the first of two Boeing 767-300ERs leased from Guinness-Peat with the intention of supplementing the Jumbos on transatlantic services. Their introduction, however, coincided with a period of heavy recession on the airline's transatlantic routes; however, rather than dispose of the 747s the airline actively looked

for customers to operate its 767s. After only a few months operating in Aer Lingus colours the aircraft were transferred to other carriers, including Air Aruba and Aeromexico. Both aircraft are currently being operated by TWA. The Aer Lingus livery comprises a dark green window line bordered by a thin bright blue band above, and broad white band below. The belly is grey and the fuselage roof an emerald green which encompasses the whole tail, upon which is a large white shamrock. The rather appropriate ICAO callsign is 'SHAMROCK'. Photographed at Dublin in January 1994 in hybrid marks having recently returned from Air Aruba is EI-CAL.
*(Robbie Shaw)*

# AEROMEXICO (AM/AMX)

Aeromexico was formed on 1 September 1934 to operate services between Acapulco and Mexico City under the name Aeronaves de Mexico. During the 1950s the company expanded with the acquisition of a number of other carriers. The first service to the USA was inaugurated in December 1957 with Bristol Britannias. Douglas DC-8s were the first long-range jets acquired, and the airline adopted its present title early in 1972. Outside of the Americas the only destinations served are Frankfurt, Madrid and Paris with Boeing 767s and DC-10s, the former comprising two -200ERs and two -300ERs. Domestic and regional services are operated by a large fleet of DC-9s and MD-80s, supported by Boeing 757s. Aeromexico's present livery features a dark blue cheatline below which is a red band, separating the natural metal belly from the white cabin roof. On the dark blue tail is the airline's Mexican birdman logo and titling in white. Photographed in August 1992 inbound to Paris/Orly is 767-300ER XA-RWW, which is really EI-CAL on lease from Aer Lingus. The ICAO callsign is 'AERO-MEXICO'. *(Robbie Shaw)*

# AIR ALGERIE (AH/DAH)

Air Algerie can trace its history to the 1940s when it was known as CGTA, adopting its present title in 1953 after the take-over of Compagnie Air Transport. As with the state airlines of most ex-French colonies, the first jet used by the company was the Sud Aviation Caravelle. Current equipment comprises sizeable numbers of Boeing 727s and 737s, with Fokker F-27s in use for domestic services. For longer range routes and the high density Algiers–Paris sector Airbus A-310s and Boeing 767s are utilised, the latter comprising of three 767-300 variants acquired in 1990. The current livery was adopted in 1982 and comprises a triple cheatline of two thin red stripes separated by a green one running underneath the window line from nose to tail, gradually thickening as it progresses. The top red line sweeps up to the leading edge of the fin. The fuselage and tail are white with the company logo in red on the fin, and red Air Algerie titling in both English and Arabic on the upper fuselage. Photographed at Paris/Orly is Boeing 767-300 7T-VJI. The ICAO callsign is 'AIR ALGERIE'. *(Robbie Shaw)*

# AIR ARUBA (FQ/ARU)

Air Aruba is the state airline of the small nation of Aruba in the Netherlands Antilles. The airline was formed as recently as 1988 with the assistance of Air Holland. From its base at Queen Beatrix International airport the company used to operate regional services to Bonaire, Caracas, Las Piedras and Maracaibo using three NAMC YS-11s. Like a leased Boeing 757 these have since been disposed of in favour of two McDonnell-Douglas MD-88s, which also venture further afield, including services to the USA. Direct services to Amsterdam were undertaken by Boeing 767 aircraft, leased from carriers such as Aer Lingus, Air New Zealand and Britannia Airways. However Air Aruba has recently discontinued this service, and the route is currently operated by KLM using newly delivered MD-11 aircraft. The Air Aruba livery comprises a double cheatline of light and dark blue, with an intertwined stylised 'AA' in the same colours on the fin. The airline's ICAO callsign is 'ARUBA'. Photographed in 1992 is Boeing 767-200ER G-BYAA leased from Britannia Airways. *(Robbie Shaw)*

## AIR CANADA (AC/ACA)

Formed as Trans Canada Airlines in 1937, the airline commenced services between Vancouver and nearby Seattle, with transcontinental services to Toronto the following year. During the 1960s the airline operated a significant number of Vickers products, namely the Viscount and Vanguard. In 1965 the airline became Air Canada and, in addition to the large network throughout Canada and North America, the company had a strong presence across the Atlantic. A fleet of DC-9s acquired from 1967 onwards still soldier on, though the fleet of Boeing 727s has been disposed of as sufficient numbers of A-320s have been delivered. The company is in the process of receiving Canadair Regional Jets for some cross-border and domestic services, whilst Boeing 767s are used for transcontinental and international services in support of 747 Jumbos. Air Canada announced a new livery early in 1994, prior to which the colour scheme had remained virtually unchanged for many years. A red cheatline ran the length of the fuselage separating the grey belly from the white cabin top, though in recent years a second band in a darker shade of red was added below the cheatline. The company's logo of a white maple leaf within a circle was prominent on the red fin. Photographed on final approach to runway 24R at Toronto is Boeing 767-200 C-GAUE. *(Robbie Shaw)*

To make up for a shortfall in capacity the airline took an almost unprecedented step of putting back into service three Lockheed Tristars which had been stored in the Arizona desert. These have been painted in the airline's new livery of an all-white fuselage with red titling, with a large red maple leaf on a dark green fin, though it has to be said the dark green appears more like black. Air Canada has twenty-one Boeing 767-200s, nine of which are ER variants. Six series -300ERs are on order, and although the airline wanted to find a buyer for these machines, the first has already entered service. The aircraft in question, C-FMWP is illustrated above taxiing for departure at London/Heathrow. The ICAO callsign is 'AIR CANADA'. *(Robbie Shaw)*

# AIR CHINA (CA/CCA)

Air China is the designated national airline of the People's Republic of China, and from its main base at Beijing (Peking), operates both domestic and international services. Until a few years ago the airline was known as C.A.A.C. – Civil Aviation Administration of China, which was, and still is the regulatory body, and which now oversees the growing number of emerging airlines in China. The Air China fleet is predominantly Boeing aircraft, supported by a small number of YUN-7s and BAe146s. The fleet of Boeings comprises 707s, 737s, 747s and 767s. The latter includes six series -200ERs and two -300s, with a further two on order. The Air China livery is identical to the former C.A.A.C. one, apart from the tail where a red logo in the form of a stylised dragon's head has replaced the large Chinese flag; the remainder being the familiar blue cheatline separating the white fuselage from the grey belly. Photographed on approach to Hong Kong's Kai Tak airport is 767-300 B-2557. The ICAO callsign is 'AIR CHINA'. *(Robbie Shaw)*

## AIR EUROPE ITALY (PE/AEL)

Air Europe Italy was formed in late 1989 and was previously a member of the Airlines of Europe Group. Despite the demise of UK-based Air Europe the Italian company continued to operate with its fleet of Boeing 757s. However these have since been disposed of in favour of 767s, as the company concentrates on long-haul charters to North America and the Caribbean. Two 767-300ER aircraft were leased from SAS, however these aircraft have since been disposed of in favour of aircraft from a leasing company. The airline has the same livery as Air Europa of Spain, namely a broad cheatline in varying shades of red and orange running below the window line then sweeping up the tail, with the remainder of the aircraft being white. The titling on the upper fuselage and tail is in black. Photographed at a rainswept Toronto is 767-300ER I-AEJC, which was formerly, and has since returned to SAS as LN-RCB *Astrid Viking*. The ICAO callsign is 'AIR EUROPE'. *(Robbie Shaw)*

# AIR FRANCE (AF/AFR)

Air France is an airline in dire trouble with crippling debts, and despite the protests of unfair competition the EC has approved a French government aid package which amounts to more money than that owed by all the major European airlines together. Hardly surprising then that other major European airlines are voicing their opposition to the decision. The French national carrier has taken over UTA, and looks set to do the same with Air Inter, thereby eliminating most of the domestic competition at a stroke. For domestic and European services Boeing 737s and Airbus A-320s are used, supported by the larger A-300 and A-310. A large fleet of Boeing 747s is used on intercontinental services, supported by A-340s, including some leased from Sabena. A small number of

DC-10s and Boeing 767s augment the long-haul fleet, with the latter primarily used on thinner North American routes, whilst the Concorde is still used on the Paris–New York route. The 767 fleet comprises two -200ER variants, both of which are leased to Balkan Bulgarian Airlines, with six -300ER variants used on some transatlantic routes. The Air France livery features an all-white fuselage with blue titling, whilst the tail is encompassed with blue, white and red tricolour stripes of varying widths. Photographed climbing out of Toronto's Lester B. Pearson International airport is 767-300ER F-GHGH. The ICAO callsign is 'AIR FRANCE'.
*(Robbie Shaw)*

## AIR HOLLAND (GG/AHR)

From its base at Amsterdam's Schiphol airport Air Holland operates inclusive tour charter flights to the sunnier climes of the Mediterranean and Canary Islands, using a fleet of two Boeing 737-300s and two 757s. Although it once operated the 767 this type has since been disposed of. Air Holland enjoys a close working relationship with El Al Israeli airlines, and operates some flights for El Al on Saturdays, the Israeli Sabbath Day when the national carrier is not permitted to operate. One of Air Holland's 757s is currently operated on behalf of Arkia, a subsidiary of El Al. The pleasing Air Holland livery is a white fuselage bisected by a double cheatline of blue (upper) and orange (lower), with two vertical stripes in the same colours on a white fin. Photographed about to land at Athens is 767-200ER G-BRIF, which at the time was leased from Britannia Airways. The ICAO callsign is 'ORANGE'. *(Robbie Shaw)*

# AIR MAURITIUS (MK/MAU)

Since forming in 1967 Air Mauritius has gradually expanded, and during 1994 took delivery of the first two of five Airbus A-340s on order. These will replace the airline's three Boeing 747SPs, and perhaps at a later date the two 767-200ERs. The airline has gradually expanded its route network eastwards to include Hong Kong, an extension of its Kuala Lumpur and Singapore service. In Europe the airline's aircraft can be seen at Frankfurt, Geneva, London, Munich, Paris, Rome and Zurich. The airline's livery has a white fuselage bisected by a red cheatline at window level, with a red pinstripe lower down at wing root level and bold red titling on the cabin roof. The fin is predominantly red, apart from two vertical white lines at the trailing edge and a broader horizontal one midway up, within which is the red stylised falcon motif. This motif is also repeated on the white engine nacelles. Photographed inbound to London/Heathrow is 767-20ER 3B-NAK *City of Curepipe*. The ICAO callsign is 'AIR MAURITIUS'. *(Robbie Shaw)*

## AIR NEW ZEALAND (NZ/ANZ)

The present Air New Zealand was the result of a merger in 1978 of an airline with the same name and New Zealand National Airways Corporation. Known as the 'Pride of the Pacific' the airline naturally concentrates on the home market and within Australasia. Trans-Tasman, regional and US services are operated by Boeing 767s and 747-200s, with 747-400s being used to the sole European destinations of Frankfurt and London via Los Angeles. On 24 November 1994 the airline switched its London gateway from Gatwick to Heathrow in a bid to increase yield, even though Gatwick flights were invariably full. The airline currently has three 747-400s with one more on order, though at the time of writing is preparing to take on lease two former Varig 747-400s. These aircraft are required to increase capacity on services to the US, thanks to Continental Airlines decision in late

1993 to withdraw from all Australasian services. Internal services are operated by Boeing 737-200s, supported by EMB110s, SF340s and Metroliners operated by Air Nelson and Eagle Air under the Air New Zealand Link banner. The livery has twin cheatlines of deep blue and turquoise on a white fuselage, with the belly being grey or natural metal. The fin is blue with turquoise trimming, with the large Maori symbol known as a Koru. Blue titling and national flag appear on the forward upper fuselage. The 767 fleet comprises seven -200ER variants and three -300ERs, with a further four of the latter on order. Illustrated is -200ER ZK-NBA *Aotearoa*. The ICAO callsign is 'NEW ZEALAND'. *(Robbie Shaw)*

# AIR PACIFIC (FJ/FJI)

Air Pacific which, until 1971, was known as Fiji Airways is the international airline of the island state of Fiji. The aspiring carrier is gradually increasing its share of traffic between the idyllic South Sea islands and Australasian destinations. The airline's fleet comprises just three Boeing products, with single examples of the 737-500, 767-200ER and 747-200, the latter on lease from Air New Zealand. Air Pacific undoubtedly has one of the most flamboyant colour schemes around. The forward fuselage is white with deep blue titling, which contrasts sharply with the broad sweeping bands of yellow, orange, magenta and deep blue, the latter sweeping up to encompass the fin. The stylish logo on the fin features a blue, yellow, orange and magenta rainbow over a leaping marlin, all within a white circle. The company has just taken delivery of a 767-300ER in a 249-seat configuration for use on routes to Los Angeles and Tokyo. This aircraft features a minor change in the livery, in that the marlin logo on the tail has been replaced by the word Fiji. Photographed on the taxiway at Auckland in February 1993 is 767-200ER DQ-FJA. The ICAO callsign is 'PACIFIC'. *(Robbie Shaw)*

# AIR SEYCHELLES (HM/SEY)

Air Seychelles is the national carrier of the small island nation. Formed in 1977 the airline commenced inter-island services, and currently uses a Britten-Norman Islander and four Twin Otters on such services. The first jet equipment was a Boeing 707, though this was later replaced by a leased Airbus A-300, linking the capital Mahe with Frankfurt, London and Paris. Singapore has since been added to the route network, whilst the A-300 has been replaced by a leased Boeing 767-200ER. The most recent acquisition is a new Boeing 757 acquired in March 1993 for new services to Europe, including Madrid. The attractive livery features thickening green stripes at the rear of the white fuselage. The fin has a thin horizontal white line separating the red upper and green lower halves, upon which are the white silhouettes of two gulls in flight. The upper fuselage has blue titling and the national flag. The ICAO callsign is 'SEYCHELLES'. Illustrated is the 767-200ER S7-AAS which carries the name *Aldabra* on the nose. *(Robbie Shaw)*

# AIR ZIMBABWE (UM/AZW)

Formerly known as Air Rhodesia, Air Zimbabwe changed to its current title in 1980. Domestic services are operated by the sole BAe146, augmented by Boeing 737s which are also used on regional routes. The company still retains two Boeing 707s, one of which is frequently used on Presidential duties. Services to Europe are undertaken by two Boeing 767-200ERs, with Frankfurt and London being the prime destinations. The pleasing livery features a quadruple cheatline of, from top to bottom, black, red, yellow and green. Commencing at the nose it sweeps up to run along the window line, before stepping up again to encompass the lower half of the fin where there is a five-pointed yellow and red star motif. Lower case black titling is on the forward fuselage alongside the national flag. Illustrated is the company's second 767-200ER Z-WPF *Chimanimani* which was delivered in October 1990. The ICAO callsign is 'ZIMBABWE'. *(Robbie Shaw)*

# AIRTOURS INTERNATIONAL AIRWAYS (TIH)

Manchester-based Airtours International is now well established in the UK leisure market. Its position was strengthened with the take-over of Aspro Holidays and its associate Inter European Airways. With the acquisition of the latter came a fleet of two Airbus A-320s and two Boeing 757s, the accompanying 737s being disposed of. These now operate alongside eight McDonnell-Douglas MD-83s to destinations throughout the Mediterranean and the Canary Islands from major bases at Manchester and Gatwick, with additional aircraft operating from regional airports such as Cardiff. In 1993 Airtours failed with a bid to take-over rival Owners Abroad and its airline Air 2000. This has not stopped the company expanding further afield into the long-haul market with the acquisition of two Boeing 767-300ERs in the spring of 1994, and these aircraft frequently traverse the Atlantic to the US and Caribbean, including Cuba. The livery has a white fuselage with bold dark blue titles below the window line forward of the wing root. The belly is deep blue and sweeps up to encompass the rear fuselage and fin, and is trimmed by turquoise pinstripes. In the centre of the fin is the company logo of a rearwards facing deep blue 'A' trimmed in turquoise on a royal blue disc. The engine nacelles are also deep blue. Although Airtours ICAO callsign is 'KESTREL', the long-haul 757s and 767s use 'TOURJET', and also a different flight code of TIH. Illustrated is series -300ER G-DAJC. *(Robbie Shaw)*

## ALL NIPPON AIRWAYS (NH/ANA)

Since its foundation in 1952 All Nippon Airways has gradually expanded and is now Japan's largest carrier. The airline was formed under the name Japan Helicopter and Aeroplane Transport Company and, over the next fifteen years absorbed four other domestic carriers. Until 1986 All Nippon was not permitted to operate international services and compete with the national carrier, Japan Air Lines. Since that date however the airline has steadily expanded its network to include destinations in Asia, Europe and North America. On domestic services the Boeing 737s have been replaced with A-320s, supplemented by a large fleet of 767s, comprising twenty-five series -200s, twenty-seven -300s with a

further six on order and five -300ERs. A few Lockheed Tristars remain in use, with the 747 fleet ever increasing. For the future the airline has orders placed for the Airbus A-340 and Boeing 777. The attractive livery has two bands of dark and light blue sweeping diagonally up the fuselage from the nose to encompass the whole fin, all of which, except the trailing edge, is dark blue with the letters ANA diagonally in white. The belly is light grey and the remainder of the fuselage white, upon which is the airline titling which, for aircraft used only on domestic services is Japanese characters only. Lining up for departure from Osaka is 767-200 JA8239. The ICAO callsign is 'ALL NIPPON'. *(Robbie Shaw)*

## AMERICAN AIRLINES (AA/AAL)

One of America's and the world's largest airlines is American Airlines. The Dallas/Fort Worth-based operator has managed better than most US carriers to keep its head above water during the troubled period of recession for the world's airline industry, to do so however it has had to withdraw into storage a number of elderly fuel-thirsty aircraft such as Boeing 727s and DC-10s. Over the past few years the airline has undergone a vast expansion of services to Europe, particularly to London/Heathrow when it bought the traffic rights from Trans World Airlines. The airline has an extensive fleet of aircraft, with international services being operated by Boeing 767s and McDonnell-Douglas MD-11s. American is proud of its distinctive livery of a highly polished natural metal fuselage with cheatline in patriotic red, white and blue. Bold red titling outlined in white adorns the fuselage whilst a stylised blue eagle is featured on the fin above the red and blue 'AA' logo. American boasts the largest 767 fleet in the world, comprising eight -200s, twenty-two -200ERs and thirty-seven -300ERs, with a further four of the latter due for delivery early in 1995. Photographed about to land at London/Heathrow is 767-300ER N378AN. The airline's ICAO callsign is 'AMERICAN'. *(Robbie Shaw)*

# ANSETT AUSTRALIA (AN/AAA)

Ansett Airways was founded in 1936 and is a well established name in Antipodean aviation. With the recent acquisition of Australian Airlines by Qantas, Ansett remains the only major competitor to the national carrier. The company is now known as Ansett Australia. Its network covers the whole of Australia with the assistance of a number of commuter airlines such as Aeropelican, Flight West, Kendall and Skywest. East West Airlines and its fleet of BAe146s is a recent acquisition. The sizeable fleet comprises Fokker 28s and 50s, Airbus A-320s, Boeing 737s and 727s, with only a few of the latter remaining. The 767 inventory comprises of six series -200s, one of which is an ER variant. Ansett has recently acquired two Boeing 747-300s for use on its first international services to Hong Kong and Tokyo, though one of these suffered a nosewheel collapse whilst landing at Sydney in October 1994. The current Ansett Australia livery has an all-white fuselage with dark blue titling. The tail is a replica of the Australian flag; dark blue and adorned with the six white stars of the Southern Cross and a Union flag at the extreme top of the fin. Photographed at Sydney's Kingford-Smith International airport is Boeing 767-200 VH-RMD. The ICAO callsign is 'ANSETT'.
*(Robbie Shaw)*

## ASIANA AIRLINES (OZ/AAR)

South Korean carrier Asiana was formed in December 1988 and initially was permitted only to operate domestic services. Despite vociferous protests from Korean Air, this restriction was soon lifted and international routes opened in 1989, initially to Nagoya and Tokyo. Further expansion has seen a number of Asian destinations added to the network, as well as the west coast of the USA. Expansion westwards to Europe is also on the cards. The sizeable Boeing 737 fleet is now augmented by 767s, with three -300 variants in use and a further five on order. The airline also has five -300ERs with two more on order, and has recently announced an order for two freighter versions of the same type. Asiana has a growing fleet of 747-400s, and it is surely just a matter of time before they become regular visitors to Europe. Asiana's livery comprises a white lower fuselage and belly, with the remainder of the aircraft a medium grey. Eight thin lines in red, yellow, blue and white run vertically up the trailing edge of the fin, and the airline titling in both English and Korean characters is on the upper fuselage. Illustrated is Boeing 767-300ER HL7286. The ICAO callsign is 'ASIANA'. *(Robbie Shaw)*

## AUSTRALIA ASIA AIRLINES (IM/AAU)

Australia Asia Airlines was established in 1989, and is a wholly owned subsidiary of the national carrier Qantas. The airline was set up purely to operate services from Brisbane and Sydney to Taipei, and commenced services in 1991. The main reason being that it allows Qantas, albeit in a different guise, to operate to the Taiwanese capital without offending the government of the People's Republic of China. This sort of operation is far from unique. Japan Air Lines, through its subsidiary Japan Asia has been operating to Taipei for many years, and more recently Air France and British Airways have formed their own subsidiaries, Air France Asie and

British Asia for the same purpose. Australia Asia initially operated a single Boeing 767-300ER leased from Qantas, however this has now been replaced by the national carrier's two Boeing 747SPs. The Australia Asia livery featured a couple of minor adjustments to that of Qantas, in that the flying kangaroo is replaced by a white 'streamer' type logo, and the titling on the forward fuselage is also in Chinese characters. Photographed on its take-off roll from runway 16 at Sydney in March 1993 is the 767-300ER VH-OGA. The ICAO callsign is 'AUSTASIA'. *(Robbie Shaw)*

# AVIANCA (AV/AVA)

Colombia's national carrier is Avianca, the letters standing for Aerovias Nacionales de Colombia. The airline claims to be the oldest in the Americas, and second oldest in the world. It can trace its history from its formation in 1919 under the name SCADTA. A merger in 1940 with Servicio Aereo Colombiano resulted in the present name. In recent years the airline has undergone a modernisation programme which has seen the acquisition of Fokker 50s, McDonnell-Douglas MD-83s, Boeing 757s and 767s. A single Boeing 747-200 is retained for services to Frankfurt, Madrid and Paris. The Boeing products are used for services to the United States and some Latin American destinations. The airline's complete fleet is leased, and at the time of writing there is not a single Colombian registered aircraft on its inventory, the majority being Irish and Dutch registered, giving a clue to the identity of the leasing companies involved. The two Boeing 767-200ER aircraft are US registered, as seen in this shot of N985AN. The bold livery comprises two basic colours, white and a bright orange/red. The latter sweeps diagonally downwards as it progresses rearwards on the fuselage, with the colours split evenly as they proceed vertically up the fin. The belly is natural metal, whilst the titling appears vertically in red on the white portion of the fin, and again in bold white letters on the upper fuselage. The ICAO callsign is 'AVIANCA'.
*(Boeing Airplane Company)*

# BALKAN BULGARIAN AIRLINES (LZ/LAZ)

The Bulgarian national carrier was formed with Soviet assistance in 1945, and until 1968 operated under the name TABSO. The airline has an extensive route network in Europe, and is also well established in Africa and the Middle East. Like the carriers of most nations which came under the Soviet sphere of influence it operated predominantly Russian built equipment, and the Tupolev Tu-154 is still the backbone of the airline's fleet. Balkan was one of the first East European airlines to acquire western equipment with the delivery of the first of three Boeing 737-500s in 1990. The following year the first of four Airbus A-320s were taken on charge. Long-haul routes, including a New York service are operated by a pair of Boeing 767-200ER aircraft on lease from Air France. The current livery which was adopted in 1985 features an all-white fuselage with red and green stripes running most of the length of the fuselage from the nose. The same stripes run vertically up the white fin, with red titling on the fuselage in English on the starboard side and Slavic on the port. Although used on long-haul routes the airline's 767s do make periodic appearances at London's Heathrow airport, and it was during such a visit in June 1993 that 767-200ER F-GHGE was shot. The ICAO callsign is 'BALKAN'. *(Robbie Shaw)*

## BRITANNIA AIRWAYS (BY/BAL)

Britannia Airways is the longest established of the British charter airlines, and a frequent winner of the best charter airline award. The airline commenced operations with Constellations in 1961 under the name Euravia. In 1964 it re-equipped with Bristol Britannias and, at the same time, adopted its current title. The airline is a wholly owned subsidiary of Thomson Holidays, and has a large charter network world-wide, with an increasing emphasis on the Americas and Australasia. The company operates more international services to Orlando than any other airline and, alongside British Airways, is the only European airline serving New Zealand. Britannia was the first British airline to order the Boeing 737, a type which served the company well until the last of the type was disposed of early in 1994. The 737s have now been replaced by a growing fleet of 757s which support ten 767-200s, seven of which are ER variants, whilst four -300ERs have just been ordered for delivery in spring 1996. The company livery features a dark blue belly with five white pinstripes running the length of the fuselage and gradually widening as they proceed upwards, stopping below the window line. The remainder of the fuselage is white with dark blue titling, forward of which is the company logo, a silhouette of the head of Britannia. The fin is dark blue with white pinstripes at the base, this time widening as they proceed downwards. Superimposed on the dark blue fin is the white figure of Britannia holding a Trident and Union flag shield. The airline's ICAO callsign is 'BRITANNIA'. Photographed about to land at the company's Luton base is 767-200ER G-BPFV. (Robbie Shaw)

# BRITISH AIRWAYS (BA/BAW)

Largest European operator of the Boeing 767 is British Airways with a fleet of twenty-three series -300ER aircraft, with a further two on order for delivery in 1996 and 1997. Nine of the fleet are utilised on high density European routes with the emphasis on business travellers, hence these aircraft have 154 business class seats with ninety-three in economy. These aircraft are used on the short flight of less than sixty minutes duration between London/Heathrow–Paris/Charles de Gaulle. Needless to say that these aircraft have flown an extremely high number of flight cycles, and it will be interesting to see if the airline will transfer these aircraft to the long-haul sectors to even out the life of the fleet. Aircraft used on long-haul routes to North America and the Middle East are in a three class configuration, with ten first, forty-two business and 142 economy seats. Apart from two aircraft British Airways have named their 767s after European cities, *City of Bonn* being allocated to G-BNWW when photographed at Heathrow in July 1994. The ICAO callsign is 'SPEEDBIRD'. *(Robbie Shaw)*

**Illustrated on the front cover**

Soon after British Airways tie and code share agreement with USAir three of the US carrier's 767s appeared in full British Airways livery of a midnight blue lower fuselage and belly with a red 'speedwing' running the entire length of the aircraft. The upper fuselage is pearl grey with midnight blue titling. The top half of the fin is midnight blue, within which is the airline's coat of arms in silver. The lower half of the fin is pearl grey with a quartered Union flag. These 767s operate USAir's services from London/Gatwick to Baltimore, Charlotte and Philadelphia, and are easily identifiable from BA aircraft because USAir's fleet of twelve 767s are all -200ER variants. As these words are written the debt-ridden US airline has announced that it is to dispose of its 767s. The Gatwick services will then be operated by British Airways with its own 767s. Illustrated, on the front cover, in full BA livery is USAir 767-200ER N652US. *(Robbie Shaw)*

## C.A.A.C.

Over the past decade Chinese airlines have been amongst Boeing's best customers. Until the late 1980s the state carrier was C.A.A.C. – Civil Aviation Administration of China. Those of you who have travelled within China will understand the often quoted other version of the initials – Chinese Airlines Always Cancel. As well as being the regulatory body C.A.A.C. also operated all services within the country, with the exception of those by the small independent carrier Shanghai Airlines. However liberalisation has seen the birth of numerous new airlines, predominantly set up on a regional basis. It will be another year or two yet before all C.A.A.C.

aircraft are painted in the livery of their new owners and, although western types predominate, a few Tu-154s are still used on domestic services alongside locally built YUN-7s. The old C.A.A.C. livery featured a blue cheatline separating the white upper and grey lower fuselage. The white fin contained a large national flag, whilst the black titling in Chinese characters was on the upper fuselage. The ICAO callsign was 'CHINA'. Photographed at Hong Kong's Kai Tak airport is Boeing 767-200ER B-2552, the second of six aircraft delivered. ( *Robbie Shaw* )

# CANADIAN AIRLINES INTERNATIONAL (CP/CDN)

Canadian Airlines International is the result of a merger between Canadian Pacific and Pacific Western, two of Canada's largest independent carriers. Since that merger the airline has also taken over Wardair, one of Canada's aviation legends. Canadian now provides serious competition for Air Canada in both the domestic and international arenas, with the extensive international network stretching across Europe, South America, Asia and Australasia. Within Canada commuter aircraft are operated under the Canadian Regional banner. The company, like many of its US rivals, is at present going through a tough period financially, which has forced it to slow down deliveries of Airbus A-320s. A large fleet of Boeing 737-200s remain in use, with eleven Boeing 767-300ERs, eight

DC-10s and three new Boeing 747-400s used on international services. The attractive airline livery has the aircraft's belly and engines in deep blue, with a thin red and grey cheatline below the window line leading to the off-white fuselage. The company logo of a large red arrowhead and four deep blue pinstripes on a grey background occupies the centre of the fin, the remainder of which is deep blue. The logo in reduced size is rather cleverly included in the titling on the upper fuselage thus CANADIAN, thereby avoiding the issue of whether to use the English or French spelling. Photographed at London/Gatwick is 767-300ER C-FCAU. The airline has since moved its London services to Heathrow. The ICAO callsign is 'CANADIAN'. *(Robbie Shaw)*

# CHINA AIRLINES (CI/CAL)

Taiwan's national carrier is China Airlines which commenced operations in 1962 with a fleet of DC-3s, DC-4s and C-46s. The first jets were introduced in 1967 with the acquisition of Boeing 727s, quickly followed by 707s. All these have since been disposed of, though the 727s still serve with the air force. Three Boeing 737s are used on domestic services whilst an increasing fleet of Airbus A-300s are used on regional Asian routes. These are supported by MD-11s and Boeing 747s on the longer haul sectors. The airline used to operate the Boeing 767-200, two of which were purchased at the same time as the initial batch of A-300s so that the airline could evaluate both types. Judging by the size of the current A-300 fleet the European product certainly must have impressed, and the 767s have since been disposed of. China Airlines' colour scheme consists of a red, white and blue cheatline, with the same colours running vertically up the fin. Lower surfaces are grey, and on the white upper surfaces is the blue titling in both English and Chinese. Photographed on approach to runway 13 at Hong Kong's Kai Tak airport in January 1987 is 767-200 B-1836. The airline's ICAO callsign is 'DYNASTY'. *(Robbie Shaw)*

# CHINA SOUTHERN AIRLINES (CZ/CSN)

As a result of the liberalisation of commercial aviation in the People's Republic of China, China Southern Airlines is one of the many carriers now well established. The airline is presently the largest in China, with a large and varied fleet in which Boeing types predominate, particularly the 737 and 757, whilst six each of the 777 and Airbus A-340 are on order. The main base is at Guanghzou (Canton) with another base at Wuhan. Although the bulk of services are domestic the airline is gradually expanding its network to include several South-East Asia destinations, including Bangkok,

Hong Kong, Jakarta, Kuala Lumpur, Manila, Penang and Surabaya. China Southern operates six 767-300ER aircraft which are adorned in the company livery featuring a white fuselage with black titling, in both English and Chinese, and a triple cheatline of blue/black/blue, the colours being separated by gold pinstripes. On the blue tail there is a red and white tulip style logo. The ICAO callsign is 'CHINA SOUTHERN'. Photographed at Kai Tak is B-2562.
*(Robbie Shaw)*

## CONDOR (DE/CFG)

Condor Flugdienst was established in 1961 and is the well known charter subsidiary of Lufthansa. The company initially concentrated on serving the major holiday destinations of the Mediterranean and the Canary Islands, but in recent years has strengthened its influence on the long-haul market to destinations in the Americas, East Africa and the Caribbean. The airliner's expanding fleet now comprises three Boeing 737s, eighteen 757s, eight 767s with one more on order and three DC-10s. It has also recently acquired a Boeing 747-400 from the parent company to operate services to

Australia, as Lufthansa has been unable to run that service profitably, whilst a 767 has been transferred to the Lufthansa inventory. The attractive bright Condor livery features a white fuselage with dark blue titles and grey undersides, with the engine nacelles also grey. On the bright yellow tail is the company logo of a stylised 'Condor' within a circle, both of which are dark blue. Photographed taxying to its gate at Frankfurt is 767-300ER D-ABUY. The company ICAO callsign is 'CONDOR'. *(Robbie Shaw)*

## DELTA AIR LINES (DL/DAL)

Delta Air Lines is one of America's megacarriers, and can trace its history to 1924 when it began operations as a crop-dusting company. Over the last decade the airline has seen a steady expansion of both its domestic and international network, with the emphasis on the latter after the acquisition in 1991 of twenty-one of Pan-American's European destinations. At the time of writing it has announced some cost-cutting measures, including dropping some European destinations, reducing frequency on some domestic routes and the 'mothballing' of its Airbus A-310s. Delta is also currently awaiting US Government approval of a code sharing agreement with Richard Branson's Virgin Atlantic. Delta has the world's largest fleet of Lockheed Tristars and these are the backbone of international services, supported by Boeing 767s and MD-11s, the latter predominantly being used on trans-Pacific services. Delta's 767 fleet comprises fifteen series -200s, twenty-six -300s and fourteen -300ERs. Domestic routes are operated by a large fleet of Boeing 727s, 737s and McDonnell-Douglas MD-88s. The Delta livery, unchanged for many years, features a dark blue cheatline which extends to wrap around the nose, and has upper trimming in the form of a red pinstripe. Almost all of the fin is taken up by the large dark blue and red delta shapes which form the company logo, and are repeated in smaller sizes just behind the cockpit. The remainder of the aircraft is white apart from the highly polished natural metal undersides. Seen at New York's John F Kennedy airport is 767-300ER N180DN. The ICAO callsign is 'DELTA'. *(Robbie Shaw)*

# EGYPTAIR (MS/MSR)

Egyptair is one of the Middle East's oldest airlines, though it has only been known by its present name since 1971. When formed at Cairo in 1932 it operated under the title Misrair Airwork, then to Misrair and a further change to United Arab Airlines. When the airline began services to Europe it operated firstly Viscounts then Comet 4Cs. As the country came under the sphere of Soviet influence the airline re-equipped with a varied fleet of An-24s, Il-18s, Il-62s and Tu-154s, though some Boeing 707s and 737s were also purchased. The Soviet equipment, which was never really popular has since been disposed of and the airline now has a modern fleet of western aircraft, which includes Airbus A-300s, A-320s, Boeing 737s, 747s and 767s. The 767 fleet comprises three series -200ERs and two -300ERs. The Egyptair livery has a white fuselage with a broad red cheatline running along the window line with a thinner gold line underneath. These stripes continue vertically up the white fin upon which is a gold disc containing the logo – the head of Horus, a falcon-headed god of ancient Egypt. The black titling is in both English and Arabic. Photographed as it rotates from Stuttgart's runway is Boeing 767-200ER *Nefertiti*. The ICAO callsign is 'EGYPTAIR'. *(Ralf Braun)*

# EL AL (LY/ELY)

El Al the Israeli national airline operates an all Boeing jet fleet, including two recently delivered 747-400 series Jumbos. Although two 737-200s are on the company inventory these are operated by subsidiary Arkia, as are two of the seven Boeing 757s. The 757s are used on most European services supported by four 767-200s, two of which are ER variants and also augment the 747-200s on transatlantic services. El Al has entered into an agreement with Air Holland whereby the latter operate some El Al services on Saturdays, as El Al is not permitted to fly on the Jewish Sabbath. The company livery has a white fuselage with a blue cheatline. The cheatline is bright blue to the aircraft wing root, where it changes to dark blue with a diagonal wedge. On the upper rear fuselage a bright blue wedge shape continues to encompass the tail fin, except for the top portion which features the Israeli flag. The upper fuselage titling is in two languages, English in black and Hebrew in gold, whilst the engine nacelles are painted white with diagonal blue stripes. The ICAO callsign is 'EL AL'. Photographed about to land on runway 27L at Heathrow is Boeing 767-200ER 4X-EAD. *(Robbie Shaw)*

# ETHIOPIAN AIRLINES (ET/ETH)

Ambitious African operator Ethiopian Airlines operates a modern fleet of five Boeing 757s and three 7867-200ERs on international routes. Domestic services are undertaken by a solitary Boeing 737, supported by ATR-42s and Twin Otters, whilst two Lockheed Hercules are used for support and cargo services. Ethiopian operates a 757 on a weekly Banjul–London/Gatwick service on behalf of Gambia Airways, whilst the 767s are used on a thrice weekly London/Heathrow service. The Ethiopian Airlines livery has been unchanged for many years, yet is still one of the most attractive in use today. The fuselage colours are white upper and natural metal on the lower surfaces, with red titling in both English and Amharic on the former. Behind the cockpit is a red lightning bolt, upon which is a golden lion rampant. From this emerges the yellow cheatline bordered by red pinstripes, within which is a green pinstripe. The white tail features the large colourful logo of three stylised feathers in the national colours, green, yellow and red. The ICAO callsign is 'ETHIOPIAN'. Photographed about to land at London/Heathrow is 767-200ER ET-AIE. *(Robbie Shaw)*

# EVA AIR (BR/EVA)

A newcomer to international air travel is Taiwan's Eva Air. The airline which was formed in 1989 is a member of the large Evergreen Group, which is perhaps more famous for its large shipping fleet. Initial equipment comprised the Boeing 767-300, nine of which are presently in use, primarily to regional Asian destinations. The first European destination was Vienna via Bangkok, a route which in April 1993 was extended to London's Gatwick airport. With the delivery of the first Boeing 747-400 services to Los Angeles were inaugurated in December 1992. Once sufficient numbers of 747s had been delivered the type took over the Vienna/Gatwick route, the inaugural Jumbo service occurring on 29 June 1993. A total of eight 747-400s have been delivered, and it is understood the London service will soon be transferred to Heathrow. To meet further expansion the first of six MD-11 aircraft has recently been delivered. Eva Air's livery is based on an all-white fuselage with a thin green pinstripe above the window line, where the bright green titling in both English and Chinese characters is located. The bright green fin is dominated by a large white globe, within which is an eight-pointed green star. The trailing edge of the rudder has a vertical orange stripe. Illustrated is Boeing 767-300ER B-16603. The ICAO callsign is 'EVA'. *(Robbie Shaw)*

# GULF AIR (GF/GFA)

Formed at Bahrain in 1950 as Gulf Aviation, Gulf Air is now the national carrier for the Arabian (Persian) Gulf States of Bahrain, Oman and Qatar. The airline was also the national carrier of the United Arab Emirates, until Emirates Air was formed to take over those duties. Gulf Air has an extensive regional network which is operated primarily by newly delivered Airbus A-320s which have replaced Boeing 737-200s. The backbone of the fleet is the Boeing 767-300ER, twenty of which are in use and are operated on most international services, supplemented by ageing Lockheed Tristars which will no doubt soon be disposed of now that the first A-340s

have been delivered. The latter type has been introduced on a new service to New York/John F. Kennedy International airport. Gulf Air's livery comprises a white fuselage with three bands in purple, green and red from the nose to the wing root, gradually thinning as they proceed aft. The same colours cover the top half of the fin, this time in vertical format. The lower fin is white with a golden falcon superimposed, whilst gold titling in English and Arabic is on the upper fuselage. The ICAO callsign is 'GULF AIR'. Photographed at Hong Kong's Kai Tak airport is 767-300ER A40-GV. *(Robbie Shaw)*

# JAPAN AIRLINES (JA/JAL)

Japan Airlines (JAL) is the Japanese flag carrier, and boasts the largest Boeing 747 fleet in the world, including a number specially designed for short-range domestic sectors. To supplement the 747s a fleet of Boeing 767s and McDonnell-Douglas MD-11s are used, the latter currently being delivered to replace DC-10s. The newly delivered trijets are being utilised on long-range routes, including Amsterdam, whilst the 767s do not venture outside Asia. The first 767s, three series -200s were delivered in 1985, and two of these are presently operated by Japan Transocean Air, the JAL subsidiary which is based at Naha, Okinawa, and which was formerly known as Southwest Airlines. The remainder of JAL's 767 fleet comprises thirteen series -300s, with a further three on order for imminent delivery. The airline was an early customer for the new Boeing 777, and hopes to take delivery of the first of ten on order in the latter part of 1995. Prior to 1990 JAL's livery featured a white fuselage from the wing root upwards, the belly being natural metal. The traditional cheatlines were red (upper) and black (lower), with black titling and national flag on the forward upper fuselage. On the white tail the airline's logo of a red crane whose outstretched wings formed a rising sun was prominent. Photographed (*top*) in the old livery on the taxiway at Nagoya is 767-300 JA-8267. (*Robbie Shaw*)

**Bottom photograph**

In 1990 Japan Airlines adopted a new livery which features the predominantly white fuselage which is rather prevalent today. The only feature to disturb this mass of white is a light grey band running along the window line from the nose to just forward of the wing root, where the latter portion is red. Where the band changes colour a large black JAL is superimposed, with the title written fully on the upper fuselage in much smaller letters. The tail logo remains unaltered, though it is slightly smaller in size than on the previous livery. Japan Airlines was the first customer for the series -300, and illustrated at Hong Kong's Kai Tak airport is Boeing 767-300 JA-8266. The ICAO callsign is 'JAPANAIR'. (*Robbie Shaw*)

## KUWAIT AIRWAYS (KU/KUC)

Kuwait Airways is the national carrier of the small but rich Arab state. The airline has had to rebuild much of its infrastructure and partially re-equip following the invasion by Iraq and the subsequent Gulf War. The Iraqi invaders stole much of the airline's equipment, as well as some of the airline's aircraft, notably Airbus's, two Boeing 767s, a 727 and some executive jets. Some of these aircraft have eventually been recovered and refurbished. Newly delivered are three Airbus A-320s, whilst A-300s and A-310s are used on regional and international routes. Intercontinental services are still undertaken by the four Boeing 747-200s, though three series -400s are on order with two due for delivery during 1995. The two Boeing 767s have yet to be returned, and the remaining aircraft of the three is currently leased out. The livery has a white fuselage with a blue cheatline trimmed by black pinstripes, and the belly being either grey or natural metal, depending on aircraft type. The titling in both Arabic and English on the upper fuselage is also blue. On the white tail is a mid-level broad blue band, within which is the white logo of a stylised bird. Above the blue band are the letters 'Kuwait' and the national flag. A recently introduced revision to the livery has the cheatline reduced in size and positioned below the window line, whilst the tail band has increased in width, and all titling is now black. Illustrated at Bangkok's Don Muang International airport is the sole remaining 767-200ER 9K-AIA named *Al-Riggah*. The ICAO callsign is 'KUWAITI'. *(Robbie Shaw)*

# LAN-CHILE (LA/LAN)

Lan-Chile is the national carrier of this South American country, the letters LAN being the initials for Linea Aerea Nacional. From its Santiago base the airline uses two BAe 146s and four Boeing 737-200s on domestic services with four Boeing 767s on international routes. The latter comprises two series – 200ER and two -300ER variants. The company also utilises a single Boeing 707 and two McDonnell-Douglas DC-8s on cargo duties. Lan-Chile has in the past few years suffered from strong competition from the emerging carrier Ladeco and both compete on a number of services, including the Santiago-New York/JFK route. The attractive livery in the national colours of red, white and blue features a cheatline in those colours below the window line, separating the natural metal belly from the white fuselage, upon which is the titling in red. The cheatline proceeds upwards to encompass the fin, where the thin white stripe separates the blue and red portions. The blue portion is at the leading edge of the fin, upon which is white titling running vertically. Photographed about to rotate from the runway at Miami is Boeing 767-200ER CC-CJU. The ICAO callsign is 'LAN'.
*(Robbie Shaw)*

# LAUDA AIR (NG/LDA)

Lauda Air is named after its founder and major shareholder Niki Lauda, the former motor racing world champion. He formed the company in 1979 with two Fokker F-27s for charter work, with jet equipment in the shape of the Boeing 737 arriving in 1985. The airline now has an extensive scheduled network with a good reputation, and has recently formed an alliance with Lufthansa. The airline has recently taken delivery of six fifty-seater Canadair Regional Jets which supplement four Boeing 737s on European services. Lauda is gaining a reputation for providing inexpensive quality services to the Far East and Australasia aimed primarily at the leisure market, and utilises four Boeing 767-300ER aircraft on the route, one of which is leased from Martinair. The airline was an early customer for the Boeing 777, four of which are on order for delivery in the latter part of the decade. The livery has a double red pinstripe below the window line, separating the white cabin from the dark grey belly. The dark grey stops just before the rear door leaving the rear fuselage white, whilst a red pinstripe runs along the grey at wing root level. The white tail is almost completely taken up by a large red reversed 'L' logo. Red titling is on the upper fuselage whilst the engine cowlings are white. Illustrated is 767-300ER PH-MCK which is leased from Martinair. Note the additional Lufthansa titles. The ICAO callsign is 'LAUDA AIR'. *(Robbie Shaw)*

# LEISURE INTERNATIONAL AIRWAYS (ULE)

Formed in 1992 Leisure International Airways is an autonomous division of Air UK Leisure, itself a subsidiary of Air UK. The company operates two new Boeing 767-300ER aircraft which were delivered in the spring of 1993, primarily from Gatwick and Manchester, with the main destinations being Florida and the Caribbean, including services to Cuba which were inaugurated in 1994. Apart from the titling, the livery is identical to that of Air UK Leisure. The predominantly white fuselage is broken by a triple cheatline of light, royal and dark blue bordered by an upper red pinstripe. This commences just forward of the wing root, and runs below the window line before proceeding up the leading edge of the white fin where it narrows to form a staff for the Union flag. On the forward fuselage is the large red Leisure titles in lower case, which are repeated on the engine cowling and rear fuselage but significantly smaller. The two aircraft are registered G-UKLH and G-UKLI, and are named *Caribbean Star* and *Atlantic Star* respectively, though the name is carried only on the port side of the nose. The ICAO callsign is 'LEISURE'. *(Robbie Shaw)*

## L.A.M. – LINHAS AEREAS de MOZAMBIQUE (TM/LAM)

L.A.M. is the national airline of the African nation of Mozambique, a former Portuguese colony. The airline was formed in 1936 under the name DETA, initially operating between Lourenco Marques and Johannesburg. The present title has been in existence since 1980, and from its Maputo base operates three Boeing 737s and two Beech 200 King Airs, whilst three CASA 212s are used on freight services. Long-range services are operated by a pair of Boeing 767-200ERs which are leased from Guinness-Peat Aviation and South African Airways. European destinations include Berlin, Copenhagen, Lisbon, Madrid and Paris. The current livery has an all-white fuselage, with stylised letters LAM in black and red just forward of the wing root, with the title written fully in the lower case on the cabin roof. The tail is red, upon which is a white stylised bird in flight. Photographed at Paris/Charles de Gaulle airport is 767-200ER EI-CEM named *Zambeze*. The ICAO callsign is 'MOZAMBIQUE'.
*(Robbie Shaw)*

# L.O.T. – POLSKIE LINIE LOTNICZE (LO/LOT)

The Polish carrier L.O.T.-Polskie Linie Lotnicze can trace its history to 1929 when it was formed to take over the operations of Aero and Aerolot. The airline ceased to operate during the Second World War, and after the cessation of hostilities services recommenced using Soviet-built equipment such as the Antonov An-24, Ilyushin IL-18 and IL-62 and Tupolev Tu-134 and Tu-154. The latter two types are still in use on European services, supported by recently delivered Boeing 737 series -400s and 500s. Domestic and regional routes are undertaken by ATR-72s while three Boeing 767s, the first western type to be acquired, are used on transatlantic services. Two Boeing 767-200ER variants were delivered in April and May of 1989 with a single 767-300ER following in August 1990. The airline's colour scheme is based on a white fuselage with a dark blue cheatline which stops just forward of the wing, where the large letters 'LOT' appear. The dark blue fin contains a white disc within which is the company stylised Crane motif. An elongated Polish flag runs rearwards from the top of the disc. The dark blue titling on the cabin roof is in Polish on the starboard side and English on the port side. The ICAO callsign is simply 'LOT'. Illustrated at Toronto's Lester B Pearson International airport is Boeing 767-200ER SP-LOA *Gniezeno*. *(Robbie Shaw)*

On 31 December 1993 L.O.T.'s sole 767-300ER SP-LPA was damaged in a heavy landing at Warsaw which put the aircraft out of service for many months. To rectify the shortfall in capacity the airline leased an Air New Zealand Boeing 767-200ER for the 1994 summer season, during which time the aircraft flew in hybrid markings of Air New Zealand cheatline with L.O.T. titling and tail markings. The latter superimposed over the Air New Zealand markings. The aircraft was predominantly used on the Warsaw–Toronto route and it was from the Canadian airport's runway that ZK-NBJ was photographed seconds after rotation. *(Robbie Shaw)*

## L.T.U. SUD INTERNATIONAL AIRWAYS (LTS)

Munich-based L.T.U. Sud International Airways is a sister company to well known Dusseldorf-based L.T.U. The airline which commenced operations in 1983 used to be known as Lufttransport Sud (L.T.S.) until it changed to its present title in 1988. The company operates inclusive tour charter flights to the well known and popular resorts of Southern Europe and the Canaries, but also ventures further afield to the Caribbean, Indian Ocean and Asia. The airline's fleet comprises thirteen Boeing products, nine 757s supported by four 767-300ERs. Prior to the re-naming, the company livery was white, light and dark blue. With the change in title came a new livery which bears more than a passing resemblance to that of its sister company. The scheme is based on a bold red except for the white cabin roof and a below the window cheatline. White 'LTU' titles appear on the fin with full 'LTU Sud' titles in white on the lower forward fuselage, while the engine cowlings are grey. The ICAO callsign is 'LTS', unchanged from its previous identity. Photographed at Dusseldorf is Boeing 767-300ER D-AMUS. *(Iain Logan)*

# LUFTHANSA (LH/DLH)

The German national carrier has an increasingly modern fleet of Airbus and Boeing products. Its sizeable Airbus fleet of A-300s, A-310s and A-320s is now being supplemented by A-321s, nine of which have been delivered out of an initial twenty on order. The long range A-340 is now well established and supplements the Boeing 747s on intercontinental routes. Backbone of the fleet is the Boeing 737, over 100 of which are in service. Lufthansa operates just one Boeing 767, a series -300ER it received from its charter subsidiary Condor, who now operate one of the parent company's Boeing 747-400 aircraft on routes to Australasia. Lufthansa's present livery is dominated by the all-white fuselage interrupted only by the bold dark blue titling, while the belly and engine nacelles are grey. The dark blue tail has a yellow circle within which is the company stylised flying crane motif. The sole 767, D-ABUC is illustrated on approach to Frankfurt. The ICAO callsign is 'LUFTHANSA'.
*(Ralf Braun)*

## MALEV (MA/MAH)

The Hungarian national carrier Malev was one of the first East European airlines to break with tradition when, in the late 1980s, it acquired western equipment in the shape of a BAe146 and Boeing 737s and 767s. The airline commenced operations in 1946 under the name Maszovlet, changing to its present title in 1954. Of the Soviet-built equipment the small number of Yak-40s have been disposed of, and Fokker F-70s have been ordered as replacements for the ageing Tupolev Tu-134s. Tupolev Tu-154s still form the backbone of the fleet supported by the 737s, whilst two 767-200ER aircraft are used on transatlantic routes to New York and Toronto. Malev has recently formed a strategic alliance with Alitalia, and the New York

service routes via Rome, whilst 'Alitalia partner' titles appear on the forward port fuselage of all the aircraft in the airline's fleet. The current livery, introduced in late 1990 is based on a white fuselage apart from the rear portion and the tip of the nose which are dark blue. The dark blue extends upwards to cover the whole of the fin, upon which are three diagonal stripes in the colours of the national flag, red, white and green. Dark blue titling appears on the upper forward fuselage. The ICAO callsign is 'MALEV'. Illustrated taxying for departure at Budapest's Ferihegy airport bound for New York is 767-200ER HA-LHB. *(Robbie Shaw)*

## MARTINAIR (MP/MPH)

Formed in 1954 as Martin's Air Charter using a single DC-3, Martinair Holland is now a major carrier operating both transatlantic scheduled and inclusive tour charter flights. From its humble beginnings the company built up its charter network operating aircraft such as the Convair 440, Douglas DC-7 and DC-8. From its Amsterdam/Schiphol base the airline operates to the main European holiday destinations as well as to North America and the Far East. The company is about to dispose of two DC-10s to the Royal Netherlands Air Force who will convert them into tanker aircraft. This leaves Martinair with a fleet of one A-310, three Boeing 747s and six 767-300ERs, one of which is leased to Lauda Air. The company also has four MD-11s on order for delivery during the first quarter of 1995. The colour scheme consists of a broad orange cheatline along the fuselage, the lower half of which is natural metal or grey, depending on aircraft type. The remainder of the fuselage is white with black titling, from which the word 'Holland' has recently been omitted. The reason for this omission is that when the aircraft is parked at the terminal with a jetty attached only the words 'Air Holland', the name of a competitor, are visible! The aircraft tail is white with a stylised orange 'M' logo. Photographed as it rotates from Schiphol's runway is 767-300ER PH-MCG named *Prince Johan Friso*. The ICAO callsign is 'MARTINAIR'. *(Robbie Shaw)*

# PIEDMONT

Piedmont Airlines was formed in mid-1940 at Winston-Salem, North Carolina. By the 1980s it had an extensive route network covering the eastern United States, with hubs at Baltimore, Charlotte and Dayton. The airline's fleet included over forty Fokker F-28 Fellowships, along with large numbers of Boeing 727s and 737s. Boeing 767-200ERs were acquired and used on the company's first international route, Charlotte–London/Gatwick. Soon afterwards however in 1989, the airline along with its routes and aircraft were taken over by USAir. Piedmont's livery was a fairly simple one, featuring a white fuselage with a blue cheatline and natural metal undersides. The titling was in red on the upper fuselage and repeated on a smaller scale beneath a blue stylised bird motif on the white fin. Photographed on push-back gate No37 at Gatwick is 767-200ER N604P, which became N646US in USAir service.
*(Robbie Shaw)*

## QANTAS (QF/QFA)

Until recently the Australian national carrier Qantas was rather unique for two reasons. Firstly it operated no domestic services at all, and secondly it operated an all wide-bodied fleet, comprising Boeing 747s and 767s. This however is no longer the case as the carrier has recently absorbed the large domestic Australian Airlines and its fleet of Boeing 737s and Airbus A-300s. Qantas has also recently entered into an association with British Airways, and the first tangible evidence of the tie-up has seen Qantas discontinue its 747 service to Manchester, instead British Airways provides a Boeing 737 to transfer passengers to and from Heathrow. The Australian carrier is strengthening its network in Asia and now operates a mini-hub from Singapore, from where it operates as many as five 767s. The Qantas livery is based on an all-white fuselage with black titling above the window line, and the words 'The Spirit of Australia' below. The tail and rear fuselage are red, and decorated by a large white kangaroo. The Qantas Boeing 767 fleet comprises seven -200ER and fifteen -300ER series aircraft. One of the latter is VH-OGH *City of Parramatta* which was photographed ready for take-off from Hong Kong's Kai Tak airport. The ICAO callsign is 'QANTAS'. *(Robbie Shaw)*

# ROYAL BRUNEI AIRLINES (BI/RBA)

Formed in 1974 Royal Brunei Airlines commenced operations the following year, linking the capital, Bandar Seri Bagawan, with a number of regional Asian destinations. These routes were operated by a few Boeing 737-200s until the acquisition in 1986 of the first of three Boeing 757s. With the introduction of the 757 the airline commenced services to Europe, which includes Frankfurt and London, though the 757s have now been replaced on these routes by newer 767-300ERs. Eight of the aircraft are now in use, the first being delivered in December 1991 and the latest in January 1994.

Royal Brunei's current livery was introduced in 1986 and comprises a yellow belly which is separated from the white fuselage by black and yellow pinstripes. The whole arrangement sweeps up to encompass the fin where the brown national symbol is super-imposed. The colours are repeated on the engine nacelles. Black titling and the national flag appear on the forward upper fuselage. The ICAO callsign is 'BRUNEI'. Photographed on final approach to runway 27L at London/Heathrow is the airline's second 767-300ER V8-RBF. *(Robbie Shaw)*

# SAS – SCANDINAVIAN AIRLINES SYSTEM (SK/SAS)

SAS – Scandinavian Airlines System is the national carrier of three Nordic countries; Denmark, Norway and Sweden. Since its formation in 1946 the airline has been a strong supporter of Douglas products, and over the years has operated the DC-3, DC-4, DC-6, DC-7, DC-8, DC-9 and DC-10. The DC-9 and MD-80 series aircraft are the backbone of the fleet and number about ninety aircraft, whilst MD-90s are on order. The airline used to operate the Boeing 747, but found that the Jumbo's capacity was in excess of that which the airline required, and these aircraft have since been disposed of in favour of the Boeing 767. This type now undertakes intercontinental routes as well as backing up the DC-9/MD-80 fleet on high density routes such as Copenhagen–London. The simple SAS livery is based on a white fuselage decorated by coloured bands in the colours of the flags of the three countries. These run underneath the forward fuselage stopping at the window line, above which is the navy blue titling. The flags of the three countries are located on the rear fuselage, and the tail fin is white with navy blue SAS titles. The 767 fleet comprises fourteen series -300ERs and a single -200ER, though the latter is leased to TransBrasil. Two series -200s are on order for 1997 delivery. The registrations of the airline's aircraft are split between the three countries, and Norwegian registered 767-300ER LN-RCG *Yrsa Viking* was photographed taxying for departure at Copenhagen/Kastrup airport. The ICAO callsign is 'SCANDI'. *(Robbie Shaw)*

## SPANAIR (JK/SPP)

Spanair is a Spanish charter operator which was formed in 1987 with backing from Scandinavian travel companies. The airline operates a fleet of twelve MD-83s including one leased from SAS. Its primary market is bringing tourists from Northern Europe, particularly Scandinavia, to its island bases of Las Palmas and Palma. In 1991 two Boeing 767-300ER aircraft were acquired and these are primarily used on services to the US, Mexico and the Caribbean. The rather plain livery is based on an all-white scheme, broken only by large bold navy-blue titling on the forward fuselage and sand and navy-blue wave type logo on the fin. The 767s are named after the two island groups the company operates from: *Balearics* and *Canarias*. The latter is painted on the nose of EC-FHA seen here against darkening skies and a rainbow as it lines up on the runway at Gatwick for a flight to Madrid. The ICAO callsign is 'SUNWING'.
*(Robbie Shaw)*

# TACA INTERNATIONAL AIRLINES (TA/TAI)

The national airline of El Salvador is TACA International Airlines, the initials standing for Transportes Aereos Centro Americanos. The airline was formed in 1939 and from its San Salvador base operates to most Central American countries and seven US destinations using an all Boeing fleet, comprising twelve 737s and two 767s. The latter aircraft comprise one -200ER and one -300ER which are leased and acquired for use to the US destinations. The airline also had another 767, a series -200 acquired in May 1986. However, this aircraft is presently under repair having suffered a landing accident at Guatemala City in April 1993. The aircraft over-ran the runway and crashed into houses, fortunately all 213 passengers and nine crew survived, though some occupants of the houses were amongst the injured. This was only the second accident to befall the 767. The attractive livery features a triple cheatline of, from top to bottom, navy-blue, red and yellow, which sweeps up onto the tail. On the navy-blue portion are the bold white titles. The remainder of the aircraft is white, with a colourful stylised parrot logo on the cabin roof. Photographed at Miami prior to its accident is Boeing 767-200 N767TA. The ICAO callsign is 'TACA'. *(Robbie Shaw)*

## TAESA (TRANSPORTES AEREOS EJECUTIVOS SA) (GD/TEJ)

TAESA is a privately owned Mexican airline which was formed in 1987, and operates domestic and international scheduled services as well as charter flights. Initially international services were charters, though the company has recently expanded its network to include scheduled flights to Brussels, Cologne and Frankfurt. These flights were operated by four Boeing 757s, though a 767-300ER delivered in June 1992 now operates the Frankfurt service, and another of the same type is on order. The domestic network is operated by Boeing 727s and 737s, whilst a large fleet of executive jets, primarily Lear Jets and Jetstars, are available for charter. The livery is based on an all-white scheme, interrupted only by bold blue titling and stylised bird logo on the forward fuselage and repeated on the yellow tail. Photographed after push-back at Frankfurt is Boeing 767-300ER XA-SKY. The airline's ICAO callsign is 'TRANSEJECUTIVOS'. *(Ralf Braun)*

# TRANSBRASIL (TR/TBA)

TransBrasil was formed in 1955 under the name Sadia using DC-3 aircraft to carry fresh meat. Today the airline operates a modern fleet of Boeing aircraft. From its base at the capital Brasilia it operates an extensive network to the north-east and south-east of the country. The 737 fleet is comprised of the newer -300 and -400 variants, of which it has eleven and four respectively. The airline also operates the 767, whose ever increasing fleet now numbers eight, comprising three series -200, four -200ER and one -300ER, though a further five of the latter are on order. The ambitious carrier has also ordered three Boeing 777s. The 767s are used on both domestic and international routes and, at the end of 1994, the airline started a new service to Buenos Aires. Its first foray into Europe, a

Sao Paulo–Rio de Janeiro–Fortaleza–Vienna service started at the end of 1994, and the company has applied to extend this flight to Moscow. Highlight of the photogenic livery is undoubtedly the rainbow-coloured fin, the rest of the aircraft being white apart from the titles and sun motif on the forward fuselage below the window line. On the 737s the titling and motif are blue. On the 767 fleet however each aircraft has the wings a different colour chosen from the rainbow, often with the titling and registration painted to match. This effect is demonstrated by the green wings, titles and registration on 767-200 PT-TAC at Rio de Janeiro's Galeao airport. The ICAO callsign is 'TRANSBRASIL'. *(Robbie Shaw)*

## TRANS WORLD AIRLINES (TW/TWA)

One of America's great aviation legends is TWA – Trans World Airlines which, like the now defunct Pan-American, was a pioneer in transatlantic air travel. Unfortunately due to financial difficulties it is in danger of suffering the same fate as Pan-American. It only emerged from Chapter 11 bankruptcy on 3 November 1993, however unless it can rapidly improve its fortunes it may have to look for the same protection in the near future. The airline's route network is but a fraction of what it used to be, and it now concentrates on three hubs at New York/JFK, St. Louis and Atlanta. An airline which was once a major operator of the 747 Jumbo, it now has only twelve, all but two of which are veteran series -100 aircraft, most of which are approaching their twenty-fifth birthday. Having sold-off its Heathrow routes to American Airlines its only UK service now is from Gatwick to St. Louis, though it still has a strong presence at Paris/Charles de Gaulle. Supporting the 747s on international routes is a fleet of ageing Lockheed Tristars and ten Boeing 767-200ERs. One of the latter, N607TW is illustrated, inside the front cover, touching down at Brussels National airport. *(Robbie Shaw)*

The most modern equipment in TWA's ageing fleet is three Boeing 767-300ER aircraft acquired on lease early in 1994, one being a former Condor machine whilst the other two are Aer Lingus aircraft which had been on lease to Aeromexico. The TWA livery has a white fuselage bisected by twin red cheatlines which commence at the nose and gradually thicken as they progress rearwards below the window line. The fin is mainly red outlined in white, with white 'TWA' titles on the red portion. Red titling is located on the cabin roof and the engine cowlings are white with twin red stripes. Photographed at Geneva soon after entering service is 767-300ER EI-CAL. The ICAO callsign is 'TWA'. *(Robbie Shaw)*

## UNITED AIRLINES (UA/UAL)

United currently operates forty-two 767s of three different variants. These comprise eleven series -200s for domestic services, with eight -200ERs and twenty-three -300ERs for international routes. A further twenty of the latter variant are on order. The new livery unveiled in January 1993 came as something of a surprise as it was a well kept secret. At first glance many Americans thought it very similar to the British Airways scheme. The upper fuselage is medium grey with white titling, below which are two thin red and blue pinstripes below the window line. The engine nacelles and fuselage from the wing root downwards are midnight blue, and the tail is covered with black and blue horizontal stripes, upon which is the red and blue 'U' shaped logo – though much reduced in size. Wearing the new livery is 767-200ER N606UA seen climbing out of Glasgow/Abbotsinch for a flight to Washington. Note that the aircraft carries the name *City of Chicago* on the nose, this being one of only two 767s named after US cities. The ICAO callsign is 'UNITED'. *(Robbie Shaw)*

United Airlines is one of the largest airlines in the US, and has undergone a steady expansion in Europe with the acquisition of routes and aircraft from the former Pan-American. The airline experienced similar expansion in the Pacific and Asia in 1986, again at Pan-American's expense. United's large fleet of over 400 aircraft consists mainly of Boeing products, with large numbers of 727s, 737s, 747s, 757s, and 767s, as well as McDonnell-Douglas DC-10s and Airbus A-320s, fifty of which are in the process of being delivered. The airline will also be the first recipient of Boeing's newest product, the 777. The airline introduced a new livery in January 1993, prior to that date United's distinctive colour scheme had a white fuselage bisected by an orange/red/blue cheatline, with the same colours forming a stylised 'U' shaped logo on the white fin. Black titling on the upper cabin and a highly polished natural metal belly completed the livery. Wearing the old livery is Boeing 767-300ER N651UA photographed on approach to London/Heathrow and seen on the back cover. *(Robbie Shaw)*

## USAIR (US/USA)

USAir has only been known in its present guise since 1979, having previously been Allegheny Airlines. Its gradual expansion has been due to the acquisition of a number of airlines, including Lake Central, Mohawk, Pacific Southwest and most recently, Piedmont. The fleet of over 400 aircraft includes DC-9s, MD-80s, Fokker F-28s and F-100s, and large numbers of Boeing 737s, with 757s recently joining the inventory. International services are operated by twelve 767-200ERs, most of which were inherited from Piedmont. Despite a massive cash injection by British Airways and a code sharing agreement with the British carrier, USAir are fighting hard to cut costs – said to be the highest of any US carrier. At the time of writing it has been announced that major cuts are required to stave off Chapter 11 bankruptcy, and that they are to sell off their fleet of 767s, including those operating in British Airways colours on services to London/Gatwick. The present USAir livery was introduced in the early 1990s, and features a highly polished fuselage and a bright red cheatline bordered by an upper blue pinstripe. The fin is dark blue with three horizontal red stripes and white titles, whilst the fuselage titling is in red and blue. The ICAO callsign is 'USAIR'. Illustrated is Boeing 767-200ER N652US. *(Robbie Shaw)*

# VARIG (RG/VRG)

The Brazilian national carrier is desperately trying to weather the storm of financial crisis, which has seen the airline return its Boeing 747-400s to the lessor and enter into negotiations to reduce or delay lease payments on other aircraft on its inventory. Quite how the airline has got into such a mess is baffling, as, by European or US standards air fares are very high with load factors bouyant. Domestic services are operated by an extensive fleet of Boeing 737-200s and -300 variants, with international routes undertaken by Boeing 747s and 767s and McDonnell-Douglas DC-10s and MD-11s.

The 767 fleet comprises six -200ER and four -300ER variants. The Varig livery has been unchanged for many years and features a dark blue cheatline within which are two grey pinstripes, which continues to wrap around the nose of the aircraft. The belly is natural metal with the cabin roof white, upon which is the bold blue titling. On the white fin is the company's black and white compass logo on a blue disc. Illustrated inbound to London/Heathrow from Recife is Boeing 767-200ER PP-VNP. The ICAO callsign is 'VARIG'.
*(Robbie Shaw)*

## VIETNAM AIRLINES (VN/HVN)

Vietnam has recently emerged from years of isolation, which is good news for the rapidly expanding Vietnam Airlines. The company was formerly known as Hang Khong Vietnam and operated Soviet-built equipment, including the Ilyushin IL-18 and Tupolev Tu-134. These are still in use, but their days are numbered as replacement aircraft are acquired. The first modern western jet equipment operated was two Boeing 737-300s operated by T.E.A. Switzerland on behalf of the Vietnamese national carrier. The airline is receiving assistance from its former colonial power France, in the shape of five Airbus A-320s on lease from Air France. These are used on the bulk of Asian regional services, supported by three Boeing 767s on lease from Ansett Worldwide leasing and Royal Brunei. With the new equipment comes a new livery, featuring a predominantly white fuselage with a blue cheatline, with a further blue band running underneath the forward fuselage and sweeping up to join the cheatline just behind the cockpit. On the white fin is the new logo of a diagonal blue band attached to a white circle outlined in blue, with a small national flag at the top of the rudder. Services from Hong Kong to Vietnam are proving popular, and sometimes the airline operates three flights a day on the route. Illustrated at Kai Tak is Boeing 767-200ER VH-RMA. The ICAO callsign is 'VIETNAM AIRLINES'. (Robbie Shaw)